*Using White
& Black Magic*

By
C. W. Leadbeater

Copyright © 2022 Lamp of Trismegistus. All rights reserved. No part of this publication may be reproduced or transmitted in any form or by any means, electronic or mechanical, including photocopying, recording, or by any information storage and retrieval system, without permission in writing from Lamp of Trismegistus. Reviewers may quote brief passages.

ISBN: 978-1-63118-602-8

Esoteric Classics

Other Books in this Series and Related Titles

Aurora of the Philosophers by Paracelsus (978-1-63118-507-6)

Rosicrucian Rules, Secret Signs, Codes and Symbols by various (978-1-63118-488-8)

On the Philadelphian Gold by Philochrysus & Philadelphus (978-1-63118-511-3)

Paracelsus, the Four Elements and Their Spirits by M P Hall (978-1-63118-400-0)

The Stone of the Philosophers by A E Waite (978-1-63118-509-0)

Practical Use of Psychic Powers by C W Leadbeater (978-1-63118-603-5)

The Rosicrucian Chemical Marriage by Christian Rosenkreuz (978-1-63118-458-1)

The Alchemical Catechism of Paracelsus by Paracelsus (978-1-63118-513-7)

Alchemy in the Nineteenth Century by Helena P. Blavatsky (978-1-63118-446-8)

Rosicrucians and Speculative Masonry in the Seventeenth Century (978-1-63118-489-5)

Qabbalistic Teachings and the Tree of Life by M P Hall (978-1-63118-482-6)

The Sepher Yetzirah and the Qabalah by M P Hall (978-1-63118-481-9)

The Devil in Love by Jacques Cazotte (978–1–63118–499–4)

Fortune-Telling with Dice by Astra Cielo (978-1-63118-466-6)

History, Analysis and Secret Tradition of the Tarot by Hall &c (978-1-63118-445-1)

Crystal Vision Through Crystal Gazing by Frater Achad (978-1-63118-455-0)

The Golden Verses of Pythagoras: Five Translations (978-1-63118-479-6)

Arcane Formulas or Mental Alchemy by W W Atkinson (978-1-63118-459-8)

The Machinery of the Mind by Dion Fortune (978-1-63118-451-2)

The A E Waite Reader: A Selection of Occult Essays (978-1-63118-515-1)

The Leadbeater Reader: A Selection of Occult Essays (978-1-63118-483-3)

Audio versions are also available on Audible, Amazon and Apple

Other Books in this Series and Related Titles

Jesus, the Last Great Initiate by Edouard Schure (978-1-63118-599-1)

Mysterious Wonders of Antiquity by Manly P Hall (978-1-63118-598-4)

Ancient Mysteries and Secret Societies by Manly P Hall (978-1-63118-597-7)

The Zodiac and Its Signs by Manly P Hall (978-1-63118-596-0)

Life and Teachings of Hermes Trismegistus by Manly P Hall (978-1-63118-595-3)

The Secrets of Doctor Taverner by Dion Fortune (978-1-63118-594-6)

Vegetarianism, Theosophy & Occultism by Leadbeater &c (978-1-63118-593-9)

Applied Theosophy by Henry S Olcott (978-1-63118-592-2)

Higher Consciousness by C W Leadbeater (978-1-63118-591-5)

Theories About Reincarnation and Spirits by H P Blavatsky (978-1-63118-590-8)

The Use and Power of Thought by C W Leadbeater (978-1-63118-589-2)

Commentary on the Pymander by G R S Mead (978-1-63118-588-5)

Hypnotism and Mesmerism by Annie Besant (978-1-63118-587-8)

Spirits of Various Kinds by Helena P Blavatsky (978-1-63118-586-1)

The Hidden Language of Symbolism by Annie Besant (978-1-63118-585-4)

Eastern Magic & Western Spiritualism by Henry S Olcott (978-1-63118-584-7)

Spiritual Progress and Practical Occultism by H P Blavatsky (978-1-63118-583-0)

Memory and Consciousness by Besant & Blavatsky (978-1-63118-582-3)

The Origin of Evil by Helena P Blavatsky (978-1-63118-581-6)

The Camp of Philosophy: Studies in Alchemy by Bloomfield (978-1-63118-580-9)

The Testaments of the Twelve Patriarchs (978-1-63118-579-3)

Audio versions are also available on Audible, Amazon and Apple

Table of Contents

Introduction...7

Magic...9

The Unrecognized Forces of Nature...12

Nature-Spirits...15

The Magic of Command...19

Four Types of Magicians...21

Three Types of Force...25

Magic in Religion...26

Talismans...30

Charms or Mantrams...32

Invocatory Magic...34

Evil Invocations...37

The Darker Magic...39

Petty Magic...40

How Evil May Be Resisted...45

INTRODUCTION

The word "esoteric" can be difficult to define. Esotericism in general can be seen less as a system of beliefs and more as a category, which encompasses numerous, different systems of beliefs. It's a bit of juxtaposition, since the word "esoteric" indicates something that few people know about, while the term itself broadly covers numerous philosophies, practices, areas of study and belief systems.

In a greater sense, Esotericism acts as a storehouse for secret knowledge, which is often considered ancient (by *tradition, if not by fact*), passed down from generation to generation, in private. At various times in history, simply possessing the knowledge of some of these subjects, was considered illegal and a jailable offence, if discovered. This usually included such general topics as Alchemy, Pharmacology, Qabalah, Hermeticism, Occultism, Ceremonial Magic, Astrology, Divination, Rosicrucianism and so on. Collectively, these areas of study were often referred to as the esoteric sciences.

Sometimes, the outer garment of a subject isn't esoteric, while what is hidden beneath it, is. As an example, Freemasonry isn't necessarily esoteric by nature (at *least not anymore*), but certain signs, passwords and handshakes given to the candidate during their initiation, are in fact, esoteric, in the sense that they are hidden from the general public.

Today, in the twenty-first century, such topics are readily available at bookstores across the country, and numerous main-steam publishers offer beginners guides and coffee-table volumes on many of these subjects, intended for mass appeal. Books like *"The Secret"* have turned previously arcane topics into household knowledge. All that being the case, however, it isn't to say that there still aren't buried secrets to uncover, ancient wisdom being ignored and forgotten mysteries to be explored. In fact, it is often that we are only able to further our own studies by standing on the shoulders of these disappearing giants.

Lamp of Trismegistus is doing its part to help preserve humanity's esoteric history by making some of these classics available to those students who are seeking to unearth the knowledge of these ancient colossi.

So, be sure to check other titles from our *Esoteric Classics* series, as well as our *Occult Fiction, Theosophical Classics, Foundations of Freemasonry Series, Supernatural Fiction, Paranormal Research Series, Studies in Buddhism* and our *Christian Apocrypha Series.* You can also download the audio versions of most of these titles from Amazon, Apple or Audible, for learning on the go.

USING WHITE AND BLACK MAGIC

MAGIC

The dictionary definition of the word magic is "the use of supernatural means to produce preternatural results." In Theosophy we cannot agree with that definition, because we hold that nothing is supernatural, and that however unusual or curious any phenomenon may be, it happens in obedience to the laws of nature. We recognize that as yet man knows very few of these laws, and that consequently many things may happen that he cannot explain; but, reasoning from analogy as well as from direct observation, we feel certain that the laws themselves are immutable, and that whenever anything to us inexplicable is produced, the inexplicability is due to our ignorance of the laws and not to any contravention of them. Our knowledge is as yet so limited in so many ways, that it is not remarkable that we should now and then come into contact with occurrences that we do not understand. We know only one small fraction of our world – just this lowest physical part of it; and even with that our acquaintance is only very partial and superficial. But the average man is profoundly unconscious of the extent of his ignorance; and he is so shocked and surprised at any manifestation which transcends the boundaries of his infinitesimal experience.

With regard to this question of magic many people express exactly the same doubt as they do with regard to telepathy, mind-cure, mesmerism, apparitions, and spiritualism; they say, "Is there any such thing as magic?" There are always to be found those who deny the possibility of anything which is outside of their own experience; "We have never seen these things," they say, "and consequently we know that all who have seen them are either fools or knaves, either fraudulent or deluded." It is useless to waste

9

argument upon people whose minds are in so undeveloped a condition as that; it is better to leave them undisturbed to wallow in the self-satisfaction of their own invincible ignorance. They are in the position of the African king who was indignant at the shameless falsehood of the traveller who asserted that in other lands water sometimes became solid. Ice was outside of his experience, and so he denied the possibility of its existence; and just at the same mental level are the people who ignorantly ridicule what they do not understand.

If we wish to try to improve upon the definition given in the dictionary, we may describe magic as the employment of forces as yet not recognized to produce visible results. In many cases it is the control of such forces by the human will. Once more there are persons who deny that any forces can be directly controlled by the will, and once more it is simply a question of how much the person happens to know. The inexperienced but conceited man will deny anything and everything; the wiser man who has studied has learnt to be more cautious, and so for idle assertion he substitutes enquiry and investigation. The adoption of this latter attitude with regard to the production of physical results by as yet unrecognized forces speedily shows that there are many instances of this, and that they may be connected by easy gradations with phenomena which are common and readily accepted.

If we accept some such definition of magic as that suggested above, there arises the further question what is meant by the adjectives white and black? In this association they are simply synonymous with good and evil. The unrecognized forces of nature are no more good and evil in themselves than are the recognized forces of electricity, steam, or gunpowder. All of these things may be employed for good or ill according to the mental attitude of the man who employs them. Just as gunpowder may be usefully applied to clear away the rocks which obstruct the channel at the entrance of a harbour, or maliciously used by the evilly-disposed person to destroy the house of his enemy, so may the unrecognized magical forces be employed by wicked men for selfish purposes, or by the good man for the helping and shielding of his fellows.

THE UNRECOGNIZED FORCES OF NATURE

Let us see what some of these unrecognized forces are. When I was speaking about mesmerism I mentioned the possession by every man of a certain amount of nerve-ether, and also of a vital fluid which flowed along with this nerve-ether. Both of these, you will remember, can be projected under the direction of the human will; so in that way mesmerism itself may claim to be a modified kind of magic, since in it these unseen forces are manipulated by the human will, and visible results are produced thereby. The condition of the subject may be affected to a considerable extent; not only may all sorts of delusions be produced, but the limbs may be made rigid and insensible to pain, and the man may be thrown into a deep trance. So that we may claim these two forces of vitality and nerve-ether as among those which can be employed and have been employed by magic.

Another great force which is used perhaps more frequently than any other is that of the elemental essence. It is impossible for me to turn aside from my subject in order to describe fully what elemental essence is, since that would require a whole lecture. I can therefore give but a slight sketch of it now, and I must refer my hearers to the Theosophical Manuals and textbooks for fuller information. When speaking on reincarnation and on the various bodies of man, I explained how the ego when descending to a new birth draws round himself matter of the various planes, in order that later on he may build vehicles corresponding to each of these levels. It must be remembered that all this matter - alike that which draws the ego to himself for his own use, and the great sea of matter which lies outside – is not dead, but instinct with life. This life is essentially divine, for there is no life which is not divine; but it is nevertheless at a much earlier stage of evolution than the life which manifests in humanity or in the animal and vegetable kingdoms. We must then recognize that all this matter is charged with a kind of living essence; and the study of occultism enables us to distinguish between the many varieties of this strange living essence and to learn that these different kinds may be employed for different purposes in magic. The finer and more plastic matter of the astral and mental planes is readily sensitive to the action of the human will; so that the living force contained in this essence – even though it be divine force – is to a great extent at the disposal of anyone who learns how to use it.

Sometimes we read in Theosophical literature of "elementals." Properly speaking the word applies only to temporary creations built up by the action of the human will out of this living essence and the matter in which it inheres. Such entities are impermanent, and are in no sense of the word evolving beings. The divine essence of which they are composed has an evolution of its own as essence; but the entity temporarily built out of it has no evolution as an entity, and no power to reincarnate. It may be described indeed as consisting for the time of a body and a soul, for the matter and its living essence make a vehicle, which is energized by the thought-form as a separate entity will depend upon the strength of the thought-force which is its ensouling principle and holds it together. As soon as that force dies away its body of astral or mental matter (infused with elemental essence) will disintegrate, and the essence and matter will return to the surrounding atmosphere from which they were drawn. These thought-forms, however, may be capable and forceful while they last; and their employment by the will of the thinker is one of the commonest and yet one of the most effective of the acts of magic. Those who wish for further information on this important subject will find it in a book called Thought-Forms, in the production of which I had the honour of collaborating with Mrs. Besant. I should recommend all who are interested in this matter to study that book carefully, as the coloured illustrations which are there given will help the inquirer to a ready comprehension of the way in which forces act.

NATURE-SPIRITS

We have also to consider another class of entities which are frequently employed in magic; and this time we are dealing with real and evolving beings – not merely with temporary creations. There is a whole kingdom of vivid life which does not belong to our human line of evolution, but runs parallel with it, and utilizes this same world in which we live. This evolution contains all grades of intelligences, from entities at the level in that respect of our animal kingdom, to others who equal or even greatly surpass the highest intellectual power of man. This evolution does not normally descend to the lower part of the physical plane; its members, at any rate, never take upon themselves dense physical bodies such as ours. The majority of those with whom we have to deal possess only astral bodies, although many types come down to the etheric part of the physical plane and clothe themselves with its matter, thus bringing themselves nearer to the limit of ordinary human sight. There are vast hosts of these beings, and an almost infinite number of types and classes and tribes among them.

Broadly speaking, we may divide them into two great classes (a) nature-spirits or fairies, and (b) angels or, as they are called in the East, devas. This second class begins at a level corresponding to the human, but reaches up to heights far beyond any that humanity has as yet touched, so that its connection with magic is naturally of the slightest kind, and belongs solely to one special type of it, of which we shall speak presently. The nature-spirits have been called by many different names at different periods and in various countries. We read of them as fairies, elves, pixies, kobolds, sylphs, gnomes, salamanders, undines, brownies, or "good people," and traditions of their occasional appearance exist in every country under heaven. They have usually been supposed to be merely the creations of popular superstition, and it is now doubt, true that much has been said of them which will not bear scientific investigation. Nevertheless it is true that such an evolution does exist, and that its members occasionally, though rarely, manifest themselves to human vision. Normally they have no connection whatever with humanity, and the majority of them rather shun than court the presence of man, since his ill-regulated emotions, passions, and desires are to them a source of much disturbance and acute discomfort; yet now and then exceptional circumstances have brought some of them into direct contact and even friendship with man.

Naturally they possess powers and methods of their own, and sometimes they can be either induced or compelled to put these powers at the service of the student of occultism. Although they are not as yet individualized, and in that respect correspond rather to the animal kingdom than to humanity, yet their intelligence is in many cases equal to that of man. They seem, however, to have usually but little sense of responsibility, and the will is generally somewhat less developed with them than it is with the average man. They can therefore readily be dominated by the exercise of mesmeric powers, and can then be employed in many ways to carry out the will of the magician. There are many purposes for which they may be utilized, and so long as the tasks prescribed to them are within their power they will be faithfully and surely executed.

All this will no doubt seem strange and new to many minds, but any student of the occult will confirm what I have said here as to the existence of these beings and the possibility that they can be used in various ways by one who understands them. I have myself made a considerable study of this subject, and you must therefore pardon me if I appear to speak positively and as a matter of course with regard to many things that for the majority of you may seem questionable or beyond human knowledge. To give a full account of all of the many classes of these nature-spirits would be to write a kind of natural history of the astral plane, and in order to describe them all we should need many large volumes. Yet the man who wishes to deal fully and efficiently with what is called practical magic must not only be able to recognize immediately upon sight all these thousands of varieties, but must also know which of them can most suitably be employed for any special piece of work that he may have in hand.

The forces to which I have referred are those most commonly employed in ordinary types of magic; but in addition to them the occult student has at his command stupendous reserves of power of various sorts not yet known to the scientific world. There is an etheric pressure, just as there is an atmospheric pressure; but the scientific man will never be able to use this force, or even to demonstrate its existence, until he can invent some substance which shall be impervious to ether, so that he can construct a chamber or vessel out of which ether can be pumped, precisely as the air is withdrawn from the reservoir of an air-pump. There are methods known to occult science by which this can be done, and so this tremendous etheric pressure can be reined in and utilized. There are also mighty electric and magnetic currents, which can be tapped and brought down to the physical plane by him who understands them; and an enormous amount of energy may be liberated by the mere process of transferring matter from one condition to another. So that along different lines there is much energy available in nature for a man who knows how to use it; and all of it is controllable by the developed human will. Another point that must not be forgotten is that all round us stand those whom we call the dead – those who have only recently put off their physical bodies, and are still hovering close about us in their astral vehicles. They also may be influenced, either mesmerically or by persuasion, just as those still in the flesh can be; and many cases arise in which we have to take account of their action and of the extent to which their control of the astral forces can be brought into play.

THE MAGIC OF COMMAND

We may usefully divide the subject of magic into two great parts, according to the methods which it employs; and we may characterize these respectively as methods of evocation and of invocation – of command and of entreaty.

Let us consider the former first. Although it may act through many different channels, the one great force at the back of all magic of this first type is the human will. By this the vitality and the nerve-ether can be directed; by this all the varieties of elemental essence may be guided, selected and built into forms either simple or complex according to the work that they have to do. By this magnetic control may be gained over any of the classes of nature-spirits; by this also the wills of others, whether living or dead, may be so dominated that they become practically but tools in the hands of the magician. Indeed it is scarcely possible to fix the limits of the power of the human will when properly directed; it is so much more far-reaching than the ordinary man ever supposes, that the results gained by its means appear to him astounding and supernatural. The study of this subject brings one gradually to the realization of what was meant by the remark that if faith were only sufficient it could remove mountains and cast them into the sea; and even this oriental description seems scarcely exaggerated when one examines authenticated instances of what has been achieved by this marvellous power.

But in order that this mighty engine of the will may work effectively, the magician must possess perfect confidence. This is gained in various ways, according to the type to which the mind of the magician belongs. Broadly speaking, we may classify the magicians under four heads, though in a detailed account we should have to take into consideration the various subdivisions and modifications of these.

FOUR TYPES OF MAGICIANS

First, there is a type of man who possesses such iron determination and such confidence in himself and in his power to dominate nature by the mere force of his spirit that he gains his end solely by determined insistence upon it. He realizes that his will is the true motive force, and he neither knows nor cares through what intermediary agencies this will may work. He is careless, and may even be ignorant, as to methods; but rides down all opposition, as it were, by brute force, and does that which he wishes simply through the tremendous strength of his unalterable conviction that it can be done and shall be done. Such magicians are few, but they exist; and if not benevolently inclined they may be formidable. They do not need a method by which to gain confidence; they appear to possess it in their very nature.

The second type of man gains the necessary confidence to command from his thorough knowledge of the subject with which he is dealing and of the forces which he is employing. He may be called the scientific magician, for he has made a close study of the astral and mental physics, he knows all about the different types of elemental essence and the various classes of nature-spirits, so that in every case he is able to use the most appropriate means to obtain the result which he desires with the least possible exertion or difficulty. His thorough familiarity with the subject makes him feel thoroughly at home with it and capable of dealing with any emergencies which may arise.

Many such men also make a study of appropriate times and seasons as well as of appropriate forces; they know at what moment it will be easiest to produce a certain result, and so they gain what they need with the least possible expenditure. This whole question of times and seasons and of periodical influences which wax and wane is one of extreme interest; but it would take us too far from the main line of our subject if we were to plunge into that this evening, for it would mean the opening up and the review of the whole question of astrology. It is sufficient for us for the moment if we understand that there are times when, and conditions under which, certain efforts can more easily be made, so that what can be done only with extreme difficulty (or perhaps even cannot be done at all) at one time, may be managed with comparative ease at another. This obviously implies the existence of influences, planetary or otherwise, which are acting upon and within our world; and the exhaustive knowledge of all these and of their combinations is naturally necessary for the worker in practical magic.

Another type of magician attains the confidence necessary to insure obedience to his commands by means of faith or devotion. He has so firm a faith in his leader or deity, that he is certain that any command pronounced in that name must be instantly obeyed. I am not speaking merely of results which may be produced upon the mental and upon the astral planes, but also of definite and visible physical effects. We have only to read ecclesiastical history to come across many cases of wonderful cures of physical diseases which have been produced through just such determined efforts of faith as those to which I have referred. The authenticated accounts of the cures at Lourdes in France and at Knock in Ireland show that a great many ills, even of purely physical type, will yield before determined faith. Any man who has in this way obtained sufficient confidence will find his will so much strengthened thereby that he will be able to produce the most unexpected results.

It should be remembered that it is his own will which brings the satisfactory result – not the intervention of the Greater One whose name he speaks. I know that many earnest Christians attribute the healing directly to Christ, in whose name it is performed; but deeper study of the subject will show them that cures precisely similar and quite as astonishing have been performed by equally earnest men in the name of the Lord Buddha, or in the name of Mithra, or of any other of the great leaders and teachers of the world. It is the tremendous faith that gives the power; in what or in whom is the faith matters but little. The greater person whose name is invoked may not even be aware of the circumstance; although if he does know and does in any way interfere we may be sure that it will rather be by the strengthening of the faith and will of his follower than by any special effort of his own power.

Yet another class consists of those who believe in the efficacy of certain ceremonies, or of certain formulae. For them and in their hands the formulae or the ceremonies are effective; but in most cases it is not because of any inherent virtue which the forms possess, but because of the confidence of the magician that when he employs them the result must inevitably ensue. If we read any account of the working of mediaeval alchemists, we shall see that they had many such ceremonies, and that the majority of them would have considered themselves incapable of obtaining their results without the surroundings to which they were accustomed. They wore robes of various types, they used Kabalistic figures, they waved round their heads swords magnetized for definite purposes; they burnt their drugs or sprinkled their essences. It is true that some of these things have also a certain potency of their own, but in the majority of cases all that they do is to give confidence to the performer, and so to strengthen his will to the requisite point. He has been told by his teachers or his scriptures that all these paraphernalia are effective, and that in using them he will certainly succeed. The man by himself might possibly waver and feel frightened; but with the proper robes and signs and weapons he feels so sure of success that he goes straight through without hesitation.

THREE TYPES OF FORCE

A magician of any one of these types has at his disposal the forces of three levels – the mental, the astral, and the etheric physical. All of these can be directed by the human will, and in using any one of them a man necessarily sets in motion vibrations in the others also. The scientific magician will choose among these, and so will save himself much exertion. Along other lines of magic than the scientific it is probable that the performer nearly always sets in motion much more force and power, and employs much more energy than is at all needful for the object in hand; nevertheless he also attains his results, though it may be at the cost of superfluous disturbance and unnecessary fatigue to himself.

Without going into details, it is not difficult to see how a man who understands will make choice of his materials. If he is dealing with a man of great intellectual development and keen receptivity on the mental plane, it will obviously be better to approach him on that level by means of definite thought, or through the services of the nature-spirits abiding there. If on the other hand, he is dealing with a man whose life is intensely emotional, he will probably find it easier to impress him along that line, and consequently he will send thought-forms veiled in astral matter, or employ the services of the lower type of nature-spirits whose bodies are built of the matter of that plane. If he is dealing with a man of grossly material type, one who has dipped very deeply into the physical plane, it seems reasonable to employ the forces and intelligences which clothe themselves most readily in physical matter. But in all these cases alike the motive power at the back is the indomitable will of the operator, through whatever channels he may find it best to work.

MAGIC IN RELIGION

We find abundant traces of this magic of command in the ceremonies connected with almost every religion in the world. You may remember that in speaking of Buddhism I drew your attention to a manifestation of it which appears in connection with the chanting of the Pirit; and you will see many signs of it in the accounts given to us of old Egyptian ceremonies. Indeed, we have obvious relics of it much nearer to us than that, for they appear again and again in the ritual of the Christian church. For example, it is well known to students of practical occultism that of all substances water is one of the most easily charged with force. It may readily be induced to absorb influence of any particular type, and will retain this unimpaired for a long period of time. We see analogy to this on the physical plane, for we know that water which has stood uncovered in a bedroom during the night is unfit for drinking purposes, because it has absorbed into itself all the impurities cast off during that period from the physical bodies of the sleepers. It is found that it may equally readily be charged with magnetism of any type, either for good or evil purposes, as will be seen by the accounts of various mesmeric experiments in almost any of the books devoted to that subject.

This fact seems to have been well known to those who established the ceremonies of the early Christian church. Even at the present day upon entering any Roman Catholic church we find at the door a stoup of holy water, as it is called; and it will be observed that the faithful as they enter dip their fingers into this water and make with it the sign of the cross upon their foreheads or breasts. If interrogated as to the meaning of this, they tell us that it is in order to drive away from them evil thoughts or feelings and to purify them for the services in which they are about to take part.

The ignorant and boastful Protestant probably regards this as an instance of degrading superstition; but, as usual, that shows only that he knows nothing whatever of the subject.

Any student of occultism who will take the trouble to read in the Roman prayer-book the office for the making of holy water cannot fail to be struck with the fact that it is undoubtedly a definite magical ceremony. For the purpose of consecration of holy water the priest is directed to take clean water and clean salt; and he commences operations by a process which is called the exorcising of the salt and the water. He has to recite certain forms which, though by courtesy they are called prayers, are in reality adjurations of the strongest type. He adjures the salt and the water successively in the most determined language, commanding that all evil influences shall be driven out from them and that they shall be left clean and pure; and as he does this he is directed again and again to lay his hand upon the vessels containing the salt and the water. Evidently the whole ceremony is a mesmeric one, and the objectionable influence, if there be any, would be driven out by the time the priest had finished his devotions. Then having purified his elements – having removed from them anything that might be undesirable – he proceeds to magnetize them vigorously for a particular and definite purpose. Once more he recites determined adjurations, and is directed again and again as he uses these powerful words to make over the elements with his hand the sign of the cross, holding strongly in mind the will to bless. This means that he is saturating both the salt and the water with his own magnetic influence, specially charged and directed by his will for this clearly-defined purpose – that wherever this water shall be sprinkled all evil thought or feeling shall be driven away before it. Then with one final effort he casts the salt into the water in the form of a cross, and the ceremony is completed.

I have no doubt that there are many priests who simply go through all this ceremonial as a matter of form, without putting any thought or strength into it. But I also know that there are many others to whom the ritual is intensely real – men who do throw strength and force into their proceedings; and naturally in their case the water is heavily charged with powerful magnetism and a decided magnetic result is produced. I myself have frequently performed this little ceremony as a priest of what was called the ritualistic section of the Church of England; and I can testify that in my own case I believed vividly in the efficacy of the operation, and I have no doubt therefore that the water which I magnetized was really effective for the purposes intended. Anyone who is psychically sensitive may easily tell upon entering a Catholic church and just touching the holy water with the hand, whether or not the priest who consecrated it put real strength and thought into his work.

Consecrated water is employed in many other of the ceremonies of the Church. In baptism, for example, the water is carefully blessed before the ceremony commences; even in the services of the Church of England you will still find traces of this, for the priest prays that the water shall be sanctified to the mystical washing away of sin, and as he utters these words it is usual for him to make the sign of the cross in the water which is to be employed. It will be remembered also that churches and burial grounds are consecrated or set apart for a holy purpose, and there also a special effort is made to scatter good influences, so that all who enter shall thereby be brought into a proper and devotional frame of mind. Almost every object utilized in the service of the Church was originally consecrated in the same manner; the vessels of the alter, the vestments of the priest, the bells, the incense – all had their special services of blessing. In the case of the bells, they were permeated with certain rates of vibration and a certain type of magnetism, the idea being that the thoughts and feelings which these suggested should be spread abroad wherever the sound of the bells travelled – a perfectly scientific idea from the point of view of the higher occult physics. In the same way the incense was especially blessed, in order that his blessing might be showered wherever its perfume penetrated, and that its scent might drive away all evil thoughts or influences from the church in which it was used.

Mesmeric influence is again evident in the ceremony of the ordination of priests; for it will be remembered that not only does the bishop lay his hands upon the head of the candidate, but all the priests who are present converge their forces upon him and lay their hands upon his head also. Undoubtedly when all present are thoroughly in earnest this is no mere outward sign; it must pass on from one to the other a strong influence of devotion and loyalty, and help to conform the confidence of the newly ordained priest as to the powers which have been given to him. The student of occultism cannot but see that all these are manifestly survivals from a time when practical magic was thoroughly understood in the Church. There is hardly a single ceremony among those used either in the Greek, Roman, or Anglican Churches which has not behind it some true occult significance, though in these days many people go through such ceremonies merely as a matter of form, and never even think that there may be something real and weighty behind them. In the older days people were not only less sceptical but also less ignorant, and those who arranged the ritual of the Church knew very well what they were doing.

TALISMANS

This leads us to consider the questions of talismans. There used to be universal belief that a jewel or almost any object might be charged mesmerically with good or evil influences; and though this idea would be in modern days be regarded by many as a mere superstition, it is nevertheless a fact that such force may be stored in a physical object, and may remain there for a long period of time. A man can pour his magnetism into such an object, so that his definite rate of vibration will radiate from it as light radiates out from the sun. The influence put into such an object may be either good or evil, helpful or harmful. In many cases such magnetic action resembles that of a cordial – that is to say, it is highly stimulant; in other cases it is arranged for the purpose of calming and soothing the subject, so that he may overcome his fears or his agitation. Such a talisman may be magnetized, for example, with the object of strengthening a man to resist a certain temptation – say that towards sensuality; and there is no doubt that when properly charged it has a powerful influence in the direction intended.

Here we have the philosophy of relics – the truth which lies behind the widely-spread veneration for them and belief in their efficacy. Every one of us has his special rates of mental and astral vibration, and any object which has been long in contact with us will be permeated with those rates of vibration and capable of radiating them in turn, or of communicating them with concentrated energy to any person who may wear the object or come within the range of its action. Anything therefore which has been in close contact with some great saint or some devoted person will bear with it much of his own individual magnetism, and will tend to reproduce in the man or woman who wears it something of the same state of feeling which existed in him from whom it came. I have known of many instances in which such a talisman was effective – in which, for example, it was possible my its means to calm and soothe persons prostrated by nervous disease, so that they were enabled to gain the repose of which they were in such urgent need.

We must not forget that in many cases the faith of the wearer in the talisman also comes into play and contributes its quota to the effect. If a person is impressively informed by someone in whom he has confidence that a certain talisman will undoubtedly produce a certain result, his own firm expectation of that result tends to bring it about; but quite apart from man's faith in it, it is possible for a talisman to produce an effect even upon those who do not know of its presence. When charged by a powerful mesmerist certain objects will retain the magnetism for a very long period of time. I have seen in the British Museum Gnostic charms which still radiate quite a powerful and perceptible influence, although they must have been magnetized at least seventeen hundred years ago; and some Egyptian scarabaei are still effective, even though they are much older than that. Naturally it is possible to charge an object for evil as well as for good; anyone who will take the trouble to read Ennemoser's History of Magic will find various instances quoted therein.

CHARMS OR MANTRAMS

Another side of the subject is that connected with charms and mantrams. These are forms of words by means of which certain occult results are supposed to be achieved. Here also, as in the case of the talisman, definite effects are sometimes undoubtedly produced; and, as with the talisman, this result may be reached in either of two ways, or both of them may contribute towards it. In the majority of cases the formula does nothing beyond strengthening the will of the person who uses it, and impressing upon the mind of the subject the result which it is desired to achieve. The strong confidence of the operator that his formula must produce its effect, and the belief of the subject that such effect will be produced, are frequently quite sufficient for the purpose.

There is another and much rarer type of mantram in which the sounds themselves produce a definite effect. Each sound sets up its own vibration, and an orderly succession of such vibrations following one another according to the predetermined scheme, may be so arranged as to evoke definite feelings or emotions or thoughts within the man. Many of the Sanskrit mantrams used in India are of this nature. In this case the charm is untranslatable, it must be employed in the original language and it must be correctly pronounced by one who understands how it is intended to be sounded. On the other hand, it is not in the least necessary for the success of that kind of mantram that the person who uses it should understand the meaning of the words, or even that the sounds should make intelligible words will be found in some of the Gnostic writings.

Be it always understood that along whatever line the magician works, by whatever means he obtains his confidence, the forces at this command may be employed for evil or for good according to the intention which lies behind them. We have spoken chiefly of the pleasanter side of the subject, dealing principally with cases in which the will of the operator was employed in order to help; but there have been and are cases of evil will, and it is important for us to remember this, because of the fact that such will may often be unconsciously exercised. That, however, belongs to the practical application of the subject to ourselves, with which I hope to deal next week when speaking upon the use and abuse of psychic powers.

INVOCATORY MAGIC

Let us turn now to the second type of magic – that which works by invocation – that which does not command, but persuades. It will be seen that this type of magic has at its command fewer resources that the other. Here the suppliant himself does nothing; he simply begs or bribes someone else to do something. The thought-form therefore is not at his command, nor are the various forms of forces such as etheric pressure or the use of the elemental essence. He confines himself to obtaining the services of definite living entities, whether human or non-human. Efforts in this direction are made much more commonly that we might at first sight suppose; for you will observe that whenever a man tries to produce a result, to obtain anything for himself, or to have facts or conditions modified by means of some agency outside of the physical plane, he is in reality using invocatory magic, although no such name may have entered his mind.

A great deal of the ordinary kind of prayer for selfish purposes is an example of this. I am speaking here only of that lower variety of prayer to which alone the name can properly be applied – that which definitely asks for something. The word prayer is derived from the Sanskrit prashna, through the Latin precor, and is connected with the German fragen; so that its original and proper meaning can be only a definite request. Often people incorrectly apply the name of prayer to what is in reality meditation or worship – the contemplation of the highest ideal known to the worshipper, and the endeavour to raise his own mind and heart upwards toward that object of worship. But the mere ordinary prayer, for definite and frequently physical gains, is certainly an attempt to draw down an influence from higher planes to produce visible results, and so comes clearly within our definition of magic. It frequently happens when two nations are engaged in a war that each of them will pray for its own success and for the destruction of the opposing armies; and this is clearly an endeavour to enlist invisible forces upon its side. Fortunately, however, this idea of calling in extraneous influences may be used for good as well as evil purposes, and we find that many efforts are made in this way to invoke from above some help for the soul.

Perhaps the most striking instance of this is to be found in the life of the Brahman. The whole of that life is practically one continuous prayer; for every one of his acts, even the smallest, a special form of petition is assigned. Though much more elaborate and detailed, it is somewhat on the lines of the form which is given for use in some Catholic convents, where the novice is instructed to pray every time that he eats that his soul may be nourished with the bread of life; every time that he washes his hands to form the aspiration that his soul may be kept pure and clean; every time that he enters a church to pray that his whole life may be one long service; every time that he sows a seed, to think of the seed of the word of God which is to be sown in the first place in his own heart of others; and so on. The life of the Brahman is precisely similar, except his devotion is on a larger scale and is carried into much greater detail. No one can doubt that he who really and honestly obeys all these directions must be deeply and constantly affected by such action.

We observe that although the invocatory magician is much more limited in his field of action than is he who proceeds by command, he has nevertheless the choice of several classes of entities to whom his appeal can be directed. He may beg help, for example, from angels, from nature-spirits, or from the dead. We know how frequently and how readily our Roman Catholic friends invoke help from the guardian angels whom they believe to be always about them. That is an effort at invocatory magic, and it may in many cases obtain a definite response; whether it does so or not, at any rate some result is produced by the man's confidence in the efficacy of his supplication.

EVIL INVOCATIONS

That is the good side of such magic; but it has also a real and serious evil side. We shall find that showing itself with painful prominence in the Voodoo or Obeah ceremonies of the Negroes. In these the magicians are endeavouring to invoke outside aid in order to work evil upon the physical plane; and it is unquestionable that they sometimes meet with a considerable amount of success in their nefarious efforts. I have seen a good deal of this in South America, and am therefore able personally to testify that results are produced along this undesirable line of activity. The same thing may occasionally be seen in India, more especially among the hill tribes. There it is by no means uncommon to find tribal gods worshipped, and the worship frequently takes the shape of propitiatory sacrifices, in return for which the tribal deity sometimes produces results upon the physical plane. We read, for example, of villages in which all goes well so long as the village god receives his accustomed offerings; but the moment that these regular meals are intermitted, trouble instantly manifest in some way or other. I heard of one case in which spontaneous fires broke out in the various huts of the village as soon as they neglected to look after their tribal deity in the usual way. In such cases there is an entity posing as the deity – an entity who enjoys the worship paid to him, or finds real pleasure and profit in the sacrifices which are offered.

It will be noticed that such sacrifices are usually of two kinds; either there is a sacrifice of some living creature in which blood is poured out, or else food of some kind (and preferably fresh food) is burnt, so that the fumes of it may arise. This implies that the tribal deity is a very low grade of entity, possessing a vehicle upon the etheric portion of the physical plane – a vehicle through which he can absorb these physical fumes and either draw nourishment from them or experience pleasure from partaking of them. It may be taken as a certain rule that every deity, under whatever name he may masquerade, who claims blood sacrifices or burnt sacrifices, is only a nature-spirit of a low and brutal type; for it is only to such an entity that such abominations could by any possibility be pleasing. It will be remembered that in the earlier days of the Jewish religion horrible holocausts of this nature were frequently offered; but as we draw nearer to the present age and the Jewish race has taken its place in civilization, such sacrifices have naturally been discontinued. It is surely unnecessary to insist upon the obvious fact that no developed being of any sort, no angel or deva, could for one moment exact or consent to receive any form of offering which involves death and suffering. No beneficent deity has ever yet delighted in the foul scent and fumes of blood; and the higher types of religion have consistently avoided such horrors.

THE DARKER MAGIC

The distinguishing characteristic of that evil side of magic which has usually been called "black" is that its object is entirely selfish. There are many cases in which it is nothing more than this – in which its object is not to do evil for evil's sake, but to obtain for the possessor of the powers whatever he may happen to desire at the moment. Much of the witchcraft of primitive tribes is of this nature, and here also there is no doubt that a certain measure of success frequently attend the efforts of the magician. I have myself seen instances of this; indeed, I once took the trouble to learn an elaborate ritual of this nature, which, if put into practice, would have given me the services of an entity which undertook to procure whatever its coadjutor might require. Not only would it furnish him with boundless wealth, but it would also carry out his wishes with regard to either his friends or his enemies. From what I saw in connection with other practitioners, I know that these offers could certainly be made good up to very high limits; but the conditions required were such that it was impossible for any right-thinking man to go further into the matter. The ritual required was easy of accomplishment, but the agreement with the entity would have had to be cemented with human blood in the first instance, and the creature would afterwards have needed regular food involving the sacrifice of lower forms of life. Much more of such magic exists in many parts of the world than is usually suspected. On the other hand, interesting developments of it are free from such horrors as were involved in the type just mentioned.

PETTY MAGIC

It is no uncommon thing to find in the East men who have inherited from their fathers the services of some non-human entity, who in consideration of an occasional trifling provision of food will perform small phenomena of various kinds for the person to whom it is especially attached. Usually there are curious restrictions connected with the compact. Almost invariably the human partner in this bond is bound to give to no one the name or description of his unseen coadjutor; and, oddly enough, in a large number of cases the condition is attached that no money, or not more than a fixed and nominal amount may ever be obtained by the coadjutor's help or accepted for any exhibition of his peculiar powers.

I remember, for example, a man possessing such a partner who was brought to me while in the East. In this case the entity attached showed his power principally by bringing to his human partner any objects that might be indicated, in precisely the same way that such things are frequently brought at a spiritualistic séance. Fortunately, however, one of the stipulations which formed part of their agreement was that the unseen partner should never be asked to bring anything which was not honestly the property of his friend on the physical plane; otherwise a system of wholesale robbery would have been easy, and it would have been impossible to trace or punish the thefts.

The example of this power which was shown to me was conclusive. I went with the magician into a fruiterer's shop and bought a selection of fruit of various kinds, and had it laid aside for me until I should send to fetch it. All that was required was that the magician should see the fruit, so that he might know exactly what there was. Then driving directly home with my magician – of course leaving the fruit behind me in the shop – we asked whether he would be able to produce for us the various items of the purchase in any order we required. He seemed confident of this, and indeed the result showed that his trust in his unseen friend was fully justified. The man belonged distinctly to the lower classes, and seemed quite uneducated. He wore no clothing excepting a small loincloth, so that it would be impossible to suppose that he had somehow concealed some fruit about his person. We sat upon a flat roof with nothing but the sky above us, and yet each fruit as we asked for it was instantly thrown down among us as though it had fallen from the sky. In this way the whole of our purchase was duly delivered to us, in the order in which we called for it; and that although we were at a distance of some miles from the shop in which it had been left.

Many of the more inexplicable feats of the Indian jugglers are performed under some such arrangement as this. Any clever European juggler can deceive the eyes of the average man, and can produce results of the most wonderful nature by methods which are inexplicable to the untrained. Nevertheless there are definite limits as to what can be done in this direction; and for the production of many of the feats of the occidental conjurer a considerable amount of machinery is required, and often also a particular position or arrangement of his audience. The Oriental juggler has to work under different conditions; his performances are usually in the open air, upon the stone pavement of a courtyard, and in the midst of an excited crowd which presses closely upon him on every side. It will be seen that under circumstances such as these many of the resources of his European competitor are not available.

No doubt most men have heard of the celebrated mango trick in which a tree grows, or appears to grow, from a seed before the eyes of the spectators, and even bears fruit which is handed round and tasted. Then again there is the basket trick, in which a child is concealed under the basket and then apparently cut to pieces, though when the basket is raised it is found to be empty and the child comes running in unharmed from behind the spectators. Again we read how in some cases a rope is thrown into the air and appears to remain miraculously suspended, the conjuror himself , and usually one of his assistants, climbing up the rope and disappearing into space. Now some of these feats are manifestly impossible; and on enquiring more closely into the matter we find that the phenomena described are produced by means of what is commonly called glamour – a kind of power of wholesale mesmerism without the usual preliminaries of passes or of trance. That this is the way in which some of these tricks are performed I have myself proved by various experiments; so we need not consider any of these under our present head of invocatory magic – though it is probable that in some cases this power of glamour is exercised not by the conjuror himself, but by the unseen partner, who has at his command the various resources of the astral plane.

Many tricks on a smaller scale than the above, however, appear to be performed directly by the astral coadjutor. I recollect, for example, a little experiment of which I was a witness which I think must have belonged to this category. Once more our magician wore almost nothing in the way of clothing, and therefore could not have concealed about him any apparatus by which his marvels could be performed. I was asked to produce a silver coin and to lay it upon the palm of my hand. I held it towards the magician, who breathed upon it but did not touch it, and then motioned me back to my seat some fifteen feet away. I was then instructed to cover this coin with my other hand, and as I did so the juggler began to mutter rapidly some incomprehensible words. Instantly I felt the sense of something exceedingly cold swelling between my hands and forcing them apart. In a moment or two this curious cold mass began to stir between my hands, and I opened them to see what was there. To my horror I found that a huge black scorpion had taken the place of the coin. Instinctively I threw him to the ground, and after erecting his tail angrily he scuttled away.

Another man present went through exactly the same performance, except that in his case as he opened his hands a small but active snake was found neatly coiled up between them. Now this was by no means a performance of the same nature as the production of a living rabbit out of one's hat by the ordinary juggler; for in this case the conjuror was some fifteen feet away, and the coin was obviously a coin and nothing else after we had withdrawn far beyond his reach. The result might have been produced by the same power of glamour to which I have previously referred; but certain circumstances connected with it make that to my mind highly improbable, and I suspect it to be a case of genuine substitution by some astral entity.

Another curious little case of the employment of this sort of traditional magic, by a man quite uneducated and ignorant of the methods by which it worked, came under my notice some years later. It happened that I had received a somewhat severe wound from which blood was pouring plentifully. A passing coolie hastily snatched a leaf from a shrub at the roadside, pressed it for a moment to the wound and muttered half a dozen words, and the flow of blood instantly ceased. Naturally I asked the man how he had done this, but he was unable or unwilling to give any satisfactory reply. All he could say was that this charm (which he was forbidden to disclose) had been handed down in his family for some generations, and his belief was that there was a spirit of some sort summoned by the charm who produced the required result. I inquired whether the leaf selected had any part in the success of his experiment, but he answered that any leaf, or a fragment of paper or cloth, would done equally well. He evidently believed that the effect was wholly due to the form of words employed; and it may have been that it was his own confidence in this which enabled his will to produce the physical result.

In none of the cases which I have described was there anything evil or selfish about the magic employed, but I fear that there are many instances in which the work done in such ways is less innocent. Many of the witch stories of mediaeval times, and the curious tales of supposed compacts with the devil, were probably examples of the black art on a lower scale. All of this may be paralleled in certain parts of the world at the present day; and the wiseacres who dismiss all accounts of such things as merely superstitious fancy are, as usual, speaking of that which they do not in the least understand. There is, however, no need that any should be nervous with regard to such performances, or should fear that they may be injured in this way by those whose enmity they have incurred. No doubt results are produced, for example, by the Voodoo or Obeah enchantments among the Negroes; but it is rarely indeed that the practitioners are able to affect the incredulous white man.

HOW EVIL MAY BE RESISTED

There are cases in which this has been done; but it should be remembered that it can only happen when the evil from without finds something in the victim upon which it can act. The man whose soul is strong and unselfish cannot be touched by any such machinations. The evil thoughts and practices dictated by envy and hatred may work harm along one of two lines. They may produce fear in the victim, and so throw him into a pitiable condition, in which disease and evil of many sorts may readily descend upon him. The man who is perfectly fearless has a much greater capability of resisting all such things, precisely as the man who has no fear of contagious disease is less likely to be infected by it than the man who is always in terror of it. Any clairvoyant who watched the conditions produced both in the astral body and in the etheric part of the physical vehicle by nervousness and fear will easily understand why this should be, and will see the immunity of the fearless man is explicable on purely scientific grounds.

Another and even more deadly way in which such forces may act upon a person for evil is that they may stir up within him vibrations of the same nature as their own. So if the man has within him the seeds of envy, jealousy, hatred, sensuality, these feelings may be roused to the point of frenzy, and he may be induced in that way to commit actions on which in his calmer moments he would look with horror. Unselfishness, one-pointedness, purity of thought guard a man entirely from such dangers, and it is therefore unnecessary that any man should be nervous with regard to the effects which may be produced upon him by others. A more real danger is that we may ourselves unconsciously yield to undesirable feelings with regard to other people, and so may, without especial intention, be causing evil results for them. That is a much more imminent peril, and one against which we can guard ourselves only by seeing to it that no thought of malice or anger, of envy or of jealousy shall for an instant be allowed to harbour itself within our hearts.

For the rest, the man who is true and unselfish gives no handle for any evil influence to seize, no door for its entrance into his heart. If his life and his thought be in harmony with the Divine Will, he may be certain that no black magician in the world can harm him. Our danger is not in the least that we shall be injured, but far more that by want of control over ourselves, our own thoughts and desires, we may sometimes do harm to others. This practical side of the subject, however, belongs more especially to another book, "*The Practical Use of Psychic Powers.*"

www.ingramcontent.com/pod-product-compliance
Lightning Source LLC
LaVergne TN
LVHW041501070426
835507LV00009B/746